HERITAGE AESTHETICS

HERITAGE AESTHETICS

Anthony Anaxagorou

GRANTA

Granta Trust, 12 Addison Avenue, London W11 4QR

First published in Great Britain by Granta Poetry, 2022

1 3 5 7 9 10 8 6 4 2

ISBN 978 191505 100 4
eISBN 978 1 91505 101 1

Typeset in Minion by Hamish Ironside

Printed and bound in Great Britain by T J Books, Padstow

www.granta.com

For Tabari

The processes by which you come to belong to yourself or to transform yourself, to constitute an identity or to refuse an identity, were thus always tightly linked for me, imbricated each one in the other, fighting with each other, holding each other in check.

– DIDIER ERIBON

Foolish whoever has killed the father and left only the children.

– STASINOS, eighth century BC

CONTENTS

Territory One

Territory Two

Territory One

we'd been in Algiers for almost a year.

each afternoon boys no older than me
would wait by the fence. above,
shuttles of empty thunderheads cornered the desert heat.

     I stood there, at five years old

     looking through their ribs. their hands copper
& exposed like mine . . .
– how I remember it – *Mademoiselle? Mademoiselle?*
my mother bringing out wrapped bread

                green olives

                  cut apples

           pitchers of ice water
pushed through the gaps.

     Take!   Take!   Take!
Merci beaucoup, mademoiselle! Merci!

that night my father stood in the kitchen's small yellow

     Steal! Thieves! Wild!

     perspiration clenching my mother's hair

     her neck –
 she just kept on chopping. the next day
 two boys returned.

     Mademoiselle? my father
the proud accountant, in tight blue shorts

     pointed the water hose right
into their chests   bursting almost like ladders
Mademoiselle?   *Mademoiselle?*

     she just kept on chopping

3

I

what a time to be alive my old neighbour
kept saying news hounding like an air raid
warning – I pressed my face against the
warmest chunk of wall asking if he needed
any new supplies – *I'm here too* I muttered
turning the news off turning my phone down
shaking the fridge saying *hang in there little
buddy, we're all a bit emptier now* allowing
the rice to boil my windows offering nothing
*Mum forget the garden today let April do the
work* – news bulletins report it's on the up
The President claims he's on the up tonight
we'll sleep inside our new damage waving at
each other through screens & surgical masks
like children in an operating theatre
loneliness needs us now more than ever the
lady upstairs I'm sure she's there her babies
too nobody around here has seen the ground
in weeks in months years from now we'll
still be running

At the Centre a House

I reached the age where I took my best glassware out front:
the teak country bench, both colonial dressers. I tipped out

my mother's orange trunk with her birth certificate inside.
made each item watch me stamp the stomach of my therapist.

forced melon rinds into the compost-sludge. when it got too cold
too dark I torched the Queen Anne cabinet with sprigs of dried basil.

incapable of reinventing my walk I found myself governed by newts
& assumptions. the house I was born under refused to cut me a key.

by eighteen I began to prod each room with physics. ratified
my inadequacies. picking at the gauze until my incisions would pus

laughing so hard I kept adolescence awake.

it went on this way for years. I fed the house nothing. waited until
the eaves gave in before unleashing my legend of bulldog ants.

the whole time no slab no gutter said a word. when I hit twenty
I called a friend. we jumped the fence to mount the tumour

of a neighbour's tree. from there we aimed tombs at the lowboy.
hurled molluscs. horns. hot yellow condoms. chunks of anthropology.

let's burn it! let's fill it with empire! let's drip feed it mitochondria!
by dawn it was over. barely the door number stood.

the house called us in. softer than an orthodox priest
with water on the lungs. we went holding our beautiful drones

& all I could say was look. look what you've gone & done.

Futurist Primer

last night they broke into the confidence shop
leaving nothing but mirrors   the whole
time I was awake trying to fix my router   today
I'm sipping Americanos with six new interns
pontificating on the stoicism of lifeguards
who grew up in rural England with all the prospects
of a stationery outlet   in a few hours a man will
walk down a street in Birmingham to drive a knife
into a person he's never heard laugh   violence
only teaches us how to keep returning to it
irl we share a third of our DNA with mushrooms
some facts need to be written down before they're believed
my landlord spends his holidays on a Cumbrian field
with his wife who coincidentally happens to be my brother's
landlord   there they hold each other inside a small
blue tent after weeks of heavy rain   I imagine them
laying over some part of a hundred million insects
which constitute the majority of the world's biomass
how their gorgeous slow lovemaking might sound
to a swarm of abstaining termites   a single ant
roving the near-underworld with nothing but a crumb
of honest soil   I think about the cost of living & how
for now we're alive enough to fuck on top
of the earth our bodies fecund with unripe disease
in forty years my son will be updating his CV
for a job that doesn't exist yet   I'll be sat
like a bookmark at the kitchen table   stirring
tea in an easy way thinking about my mother
& father & the days water was water   a soft-voiced
lady with perfect posture will project onto the wall
of my living room via a device fixed to the roof

hoping to sell me a brighter version of myself
saying something like *we'll keep the future in your size*
I'll decline   returning to the sofa where I'll
remember the greengrocer   the joys of his old
Instagram account full of organic kale & deals
on kombucha   then before I do anything else
I'll think the penis really does not age well

Heritage Aesthetics

I'm close to finishing *The Ending of Time*
where J. Krishnamurti & Dr David Bohm
discuss the nature of existence

on page ninety-seven Krishnamurti asks
why do we have ideas? Is the ground an
idea? Why have ideas become so important?

let's take the boy who was made to learn
the national anthem before his birth-skin
who failed to remember
       words like *long live*
       save hidden inside his lunch box
behind the lockers . . .   what else can I say
about this boy

      later   in the pub

England scored a man wearing the classic
white shirt with three lions stitched on
rushed over grabbing him in the way men do
when they know they're winning

       he looked
       at me
       this
       boy
       the
       man

squeezing
him
into
himself

disappearing through
God   noble   victorious

  you ever seen someone
just go missing in front of you?

  a violence so exact it sanitises history

at the frontier four cadets pop nicotine gum
the blond choir boy with hatchets in his falsetto then begins.

Bohm responds to Krishnamurti saying
ideas are often taken to be something more
than ideas, we feel they are not ideas but a reality.

Tottenham 2003:

sirens rolled us around our car imposing
the sense of sinking – out step three
officers loaded with badge & belly
holsters real mean-looking three sets of
cuffs poking out readymade moons or
better still truncheons pepper spray rope
bad tatts on biceps nobody said a word

13

to us boys nobody said what our boy did or
might have done they just yanked him out
like a dummy from a charity box a party
cracker for a housewarming friends forgot
about they beat him wide open like a dog's jaw
until he was like the animals you see on the
side of a road waiting to get finished by
some wayward driver

     you

       ever

seen the expression on a man's face when
he fights the way he fucks? our boy
hurrying back into (where) (why) we
screamed inside us seeing pristine boots
go to work all elegant kneeing up his
eggshell ribs no longer his but theirs to
Buckaroo   Subbuteo   Texas
Hold'em   Poker

          to fold then dash into
a van / tank / truck / river in a suffocating
courtroom: effigies / targets / aboriginal
folk / ethnics / where nobody can dry their
ancestry off or celebrate how their people
rebelled.

next day they released him

& where   the fuck were you

man   ?

     ❁

I've underlined a section of Bohm's
dialogue where he states

I think in the mind there is a demand
for certainty; we want to be sure.
So there is no enquiring.

you're expecting to see
the boy here or maybe
you've built an impression
of him:

       hair type

       complexion

       race / ethnicity

       religion

       education

Q.
A: I don't remember
Q.
A: Just over two years
Q.
A: I'm positive
Q.
A: I couldn't tell you

which you call on when certain
literatures require you to explicate
your life experience or perhaps you're
working around a system of logic
which looks to undermine patriotism
& state violence which, as you're
aware, are analogous

I don't know what to tell you
aside from the fact the boy lived
& the other one didn't.

towards the end of the discussion
Krishnamurti posits *I want to clear up*
all the illusions about nationalism; I have
got rid of my illusion about belief, about this,
about that.

At the end of it, I realise my mind is illusion.

You see, to me, who has lived for a thousand
years, to find all this is absolutely worthless,
is something enormous.

it's hard to accept
that this is the life we'll die in

feeding us its uncertainty
we load up on ginger shots

knowing almost anything can
be cooked on a legacy of steam

paying attention to ingredients
checking for words we recognise

alive at the point of death or just alive
depending on . . .

let me clarify   the boy
                    should still
                    be here

living with his daughter
who would by now be
fifteen – he should be
asking her to turn the
music down pouring full
fat milk over his cereal
shallow frying grass-fed
beef.

                    the boy
                    should still
                    be here

Krishnamurti ends with
we have talked now for a very long time,
I think we have reached somewhere.

Sept 1980: four years before the boy's
birth. Oct 2020. Winter is lost in my city.
the world as you know is impossible.

I'm looking through old photos.
reconstructing. my son & I play
a game where we need to guess
the siren type outside the window.

he wants to know what I'm doing.
there's nothing J. Krishnamurti
or Dr David Bohm have to say
about this.

handing me a Lego figurine
he sits on my lap asking
who those boys are. their
names. which one am I.

in the kitchen his mother
discusses the next stages.
peeling carrots to soft jazz.
on the other end a voice.

by the time I get to say
the boy's name my son
is asleep. his breathing
a sheet. his body. his.

I take the Lego figurine
from his hand. kiss
the summit of his skull.
end the remaining light.

in the morning I will ask
the figurine's name &
again he'll remind me.

Let Me Say this Again the Way I Mean it

the man on the right opens with
>   *we're not here to micro-manage your politics,*
>   *we, like you, just don't like to see people suffer.*

>   for a second I agree.

the man on the left asks if I'd be happy
donating what I can to end *child poverty*

>   *homelessness*
>   *thalassemia*
>   *testicular cancer*
>   *expansionism*

behind both men, a fox.
clamped in its jaw, an oyster.
behind the oyster, a chestnut tree.

I've been overthinking the silence
between the moment a baby falls
& the second it cries out for help

the parent who comes rushing over
>   & the one who fails to notice

>   *whatever you can spare. whatever*
>   *you feel comfortable giving.*

both men in their Sunday suits
pronounce my name like a gift

I go ahead   loading up each box
surrendering to the mouths I close

II

We Are Us Now

Sergeant Clerk is the Acorn's clerk
But is prone to get in rages.
If the Wogs give any trouble
He puts them into cages.

          – *The Grenadier* magazine, published in British Cyprus, 1958

Boy at the back, why have you come here
the wrong way round & why do you struggle
to tell the group how many of the tribe
you've brought along with you?

I love this country   (I do)
but its yesterday is father-terrifying

  we swapped a cage for a cage
  as you do

both grandparents splitting mops & bruised plums
              Christmas '88

      that was my family   living with the family
      from next door   the kids by the barbed

wire fence playing with prayers they couldn't use   dressing
me in a flag   that was unlike mine

      (God grew into a secret way of admitting trouble)

each Remembrance Sunday   I knelt
in a field behind the house where only twigs
      found it in them to bend   a shot rabbit running
      from what I couldn't see

most of life happens behind us or has happened in a different colour

the TV in our kitchen lost its mind
at my mother's immigrant face

despite her best shepherd's pie

my father   his briefcase
made of genuine leather said *boy*

wherever you stand make sure
you can be seen

&

don't move
don't say another fucking
thing

Now My Ego Wants Better Things

evenings shoulder into the jasmine. fouler than a fatted cock.
each peony born to its station grows towards similar heights.

we write so well for our kind. license the lexicon of power
like the narcissism of a bullet.

stand by for a pile-on in snow. history's digital cache dilates.
news gets crowned our century's insomniac.

you're struggling to backpedal . . . spinning around the flush.

I'll come clean: I can't stomach these tiny screens. ten-minute
videos. someone's about to get cancelled.

you know where this is heading. some never get to come back
as *I'm sorry*. how do you look so authentic in reproach?

breath rich in haemoglobin. your smirk thick with lipids.
you know some lives won't make it the full way.

again. bodies will be snuffed at a red light.

at the bottom of your rhetoric semantics crawl.
I want to vandalise speech. repurpose each syllable with a fairer
way of shaping.
you sit sharing a readymade war. bickering over its origin. you & I
know the world is the last time for some of us
who want life slowed. each hashtag comes with a perfect set of holes.
a cell. no matter the protest our actions become

we'll be hauling our slang around like a state calling back
its dogs. who brand wounds to sell them on. no matter
the language we arrive in. no matter how long it's been since

My Weapons Are Working People

heat from my father's chest – North London
parkland sweating like ice chocs – a cranium
of thick black hair inflicting memories –
smoking slats of anxiety: tonight we're here
to weigh up streets – demanding justice – as
if each of my weapons are working people
– each politician repatriating trauma *it all
becomes political* went my father's rejoinder
– what I would add if I could hold him the
way I do these words on a placard – I never
could say exactly what I felt – man to man to
woman – our love dragging what it was like
to the headlines – I read another white tell-
ing us to go back to where we once were alive
– before the butcher's apron – a stint of bad
science + tabloids erect with military men –
lofts loaded with records – your sweet grand-
daddy probably hated us: those golden old-
ies – union jacks – relics of a dirty haunting
how does a Luton fascist relax on Christmas
day – follow that logic through from banter
when Tommy quipped – *go suck your dad's
brown dick* – at home when I told my father
he punched a hole through the bloody water-
colours of his steak – I ran through Cable
Street past Churchill's stone overseeing six
rough sleepers under the lights – *my brothers
today we're all fury – no amity – knuckles like
hockey pucks – feral crows stuffed into ruck-
sacks* – I'm still looking for a place to park
my mixed up blood – my son in my father's

lap the skin around his throat lax – almost
an outline of Saint Bakhita – I'm behind
the museum on the road where philosophy
overlooks itself – proximate to my feet is the
call to prayer & isn't the future made up this
way – of people like us becoming the history
of the way we tried to breathe

No Such Thing

call me

they buried him on his birthday

when you get this

my mother by his grave
her phone   panning the grounds
knowing he'll keep that same patch of earth
for all his troubles until there's no such thing
as us
            I replayed the video she sent

I need to tell you something

forty-seven times
I know this because I counted
            her sound   holding
her breath I could hear it   wanting
to soak   the spines
of condolence cards   her dead

your uncle

brother   I'll walk those
years for you lining them with ski slopes
Kentish Town – Moss Side – Bramhall –
I remember

even though urban kids are terrible
at knowing what to do with their precious ruins
     it's there for a second then

    died   *last night*
  air
    his heart

the absence of a body is not the absence
of memory   no matter what we do for it (this life)
    will never need us twice

III

Perhaps, a Rhetoric

What they are they were; and what they were they are – an indolent, careless and mimetic people, but without a spark of Turkish fire, without a touch of Grecian taste. With neither beauty of body nor sense of beauty in mind – with neither personal restlessness nor pride of origin – with neither large aspirations nor practical dexterity of hand, they live on in a limpid state, like creatures of the lower types clinging to life for life's own sake; voluptuaries of the sun and sea; holding on by simple animal tenacity through tempests which have wrecked the nobler races of mankind.

– WILLIAM HEPWORTH DIXON, *British Cyprus*, 1887

> *reminding one that the whole island*
> *is geologically simply an appendix to*
> *the Anatolian continent which has*
> *at some time been broken off and set*
> *free to float*

from where the travel writer stood
in a doorway to invent a hybrid
people, mining history, singular as
carob tree grounds, raising flags
vernaculars flattened by a litter of
corpses – *boys* did I tell you about
my great-grandfather who was
moved out of his body by rifles
in '74 on Cyprus maritime spirits
decoloured its waters *London Rome*
Venice Turkey Egypt Byzantium
when I first stood up to a mirror I
couldn't tell what I was supposed to
be looking at. the day I left home
to hunt down my roots I knew
I'd find ideologies trapped under

prefixes, litigating around a kitchen table, when I asked my father who we were, his mouth packed with pork & brine provided only the word *Hellene*, facing away from my mother's dead grandfather

I probed deeper to learn why that dark muleteer was expelled from his life near a ditch he'd dug alone seven miles north of the capital – Λευκωσία or Nicosia or Lefkoşa – bullets he'd feel but not see, I needed to stand over the exact patch where his blood dulled – my father, with the last of the bread, carried on mopping the juices from his plate

recent research has carried the history of Cyprus back to the early Neolithic age when the island seems to have been first settled by an enterprising people whose origins are obscure

from the Latin *obscurus* (dark) from the Indo-European root *to cover*, I'm dragging my body back to the middle, attempting to conjure the flight path. I'm headed to the village where my mother was born, seven miles north of the capital, bound in a nightshirt with little to record the light, while the travel writer reclines in business class, scrawling into his Moleskine. I feel to walk over, to blunt the edge of each phrase, to ask what he means by *Inbetweens Anatolian Hybrids Asiatics* – on landing I follow him through passport control, over to the taxi rank where he takes another look around before scribbling *Bellapaix*, I want to change it back to Bellapais or Μπελαπάις or Beylerbeyi – *boys* – I'm back here looking for those black scorpions aberrant & brazen in leather sandals, an old harbour man warns me of chaining myself to a burning rock, saying I should apologise to past fires.

in the next chapter the travel writer will invent a new kind of flame distinguishable from the last where he'll sit like a monument on a red hill ordering everything he refuses to understand

northwards:	anemones
monasteries	mosques
olive branches	snake boots

It was an odd letter from a factory-hand who was dying to know about the world and thought that a pen-pal was the best way to find out. She asked Leonides whether everyone was black in Cyprus and wore night-shirts

to dream in the skin's original language *eteocypriot* to speak up against Persians Phoenicians Greeks Assyrians the travel writer spends his evenings bickering with mosquitos drunk under vineyards – *boys* – I need you to come across the Mesaoria Plain which gave me a mother years before the war practised throwing bodies of children into wells, marched men across the sea, their limbs like gleaming skewers underwater – the travel writer sits at his desk with all this knowledge while I beg on for better directions, a little understanding, passing the corroded motorbike, the grey donkey with hoof avulsion

I'm seven miles north from the capital, the travel writer hooks his gaze to a Venetian window, to where Morphou Bay withdraws its wash, starting each chapter with a green line, his hands at work, a widow is

no good to anyone here, folding life
inside a crease, the shepherd sig-
nals to where a girl learns to fly a
kite with her father, her arm callig-
raphy, I head towards them to see
how the sun bleaches the Troodos
mountains white

but that is what these islands are for;
they are places where different des-
tinies can meet and intersect in the
full isolation of time

until the travel writer decides
his final chapter is complete, the
book written, packing away pos-
sessions, ordering a taxi back to the
airport. in the square the subjects
have gathered to oppose the lynch-
ing of a twelve-year-old boy who
fired at a British soldier, the travel
writer asks his driver to stop near
the checkpoint, to watch the noose
around the boy's neck, a warm
patch appearing, darkening his
shorts, washing the residue from
his legs. the travel writer spits out
the stone from a date declaring *if*
you kill you must die – cries from
the crowd console the same copper
dirt my great-grandfather was fed,

the travel writer lights his last cig-
arette at the exact moment the boy
swings from right to left. Governor
Harding ordered the boy's body
not to be returned to his mother.
seven miles north of the capital
I'm told I'm standing by the exact
spot where my great-grandfather's
house once stood. cyclamens now
in bloom & just there, if you keep
walking past the old Mukhtar's hut,
you'll notice in the earth a mound
surrounded by a minor depression

On the Orphanage We Found Nothing

my grandmother's passport memorised British
tooth marks. a suited bureaucrat showed up
in the Limassol district to present my grandfather with a golden ticket in the winter of '58.
their first flat was opposite a hospice where at
night my grandfather worked on his numeracy
counting aloud every window with lights on.
as a kid I promised I'd help him lift the bodies
out of water, to carry them across the electorate
line. one afternoon a German tourist appeared
wanting to know where the big orphanage
had gone. together we browsed online as a
man approached with little to say, who asked
us for anything we had spare; the rooftops now
swollen, my hands too thick for pockets, my
mouth bigger than what I handed to him.
behind the Co-op a cement mixer prepared
affordable housing where the market was once
full of berries & tarpaulin, the butcher with
his tired joke about the farmer who killed all
his livestock just to say he was ready to *turn
over a new leaf.* on the orphanage we found
nothing. just a sack of empty names. last month
they sold off the last children's hospital. how it
ended for my grandfather? in a room without
prayer, a pair of blue slippers by the door

Inner Lone Drift

I covered the flies I killed this morning with cinnamon
messaged to say I was ready. outside the heat bore slabs.
Cyprus in August punishes whoever it catches. your car idled
at the foot of the drive   –   we said nothing   –
skittering through sweeps of flatlands.   stuffed hills
    arid with lack . . .

          I felt to mention how yellow
our world looked   to disrupt the air-con's fluster.
your indicator stayed on.   I couldn't stop hearing it.
I should have said something.   last year you came to her
grave alone.   I wanted to ask how you remembered the way
          as confession.

        belief arrives to rescue us
from fact   why else do we demarcate
our dead?   at the foot of her name you left
a black bucket.   two seashells rattled inside.   thoughts
kept coming: a tap never takes   it only gives.
      we worked clumps of bird shit from the stone.

      poured ourselves over hot marble. riddled
backs defying the sun.   cracked the necks of dried stalks.
you   calling me to cup a flame   preparing what endured.
frankincense.   I wondered what could grow up here.   who would
be mad enough to come all this way to leave such a small thing
in the ground.   I wanted to ask how you were feeling.

running my wrists along each crucifix's edge.

it's only natural for the dead to appear so alike

after centuries of earth.   for the drive back to Limassol we kept

the windows down.   you asked if I was hungry.

I wanted to tell you what I'd read . . . how the suffering of a pig

can never be conceptualised. how long it putrefies in the gut.

you turned off the engine. I thought to suggest standing

closer to the sea.   maybe we could spot the flanks

of an easier world.

       back at the apartment I remembered what I'd wanted to say.

how each hour a bird will die without a word for it. going on

to replace one sky with the next. a car's rear lights guzzled by fumes.

Text Message

fail to see the story within fifteen seconds &
the whole event dies. when the phone rings
I know exactly who it is. in this new decade
the battle is logging off for good. how else
can I keep hurrying over the news? I worry
hello will soon become extinct. my little boy
remembers his numbers. I leave an ear by
his box. he counts the world in billions. my
future has sprawled itself over your last solar
panel

your future is brokering a deal with the
moon. tomorrow. this earth will be dead &
we'll be the only living things. a man I love
asked if I was planning to never speak to him
again. I lifted a cornflake from out his beard.
rubbed camphor over his knees. in which of
these great directions should we grieve? held
hostage by another person's version of us.
the boys I grew up around

never could trust the smiles of dancers. in
an hour I'll get my tongue pierced. cruelty
is spending your whole life beside the same
flower only to have it go die first. my MP
digs burnt strawberries from out his neck-
bone. begs to borrow a light. I might try
another prison visit. my cousin's back in. I
may ask you to take a photo of me standing
outside my toughest dream. whatever I gift
my hands melts my skin

pushing plastic into the centre of fish since
the '80s my opinions are back on the market.
after years of being bad being good is now
my enemy's smirk. some experts argue air
moves through the larynx to create a single
human voice   &   really I don't care about
this. I've been hanging around here just to
ask which way my life went – such a private
beast is the head

15 × 22

I'm standing feet apart   believing the truth

in an attempt to reach my brother   David-Dave-Dee-D

     enough of us already overidentify as fundamental

   the movement refuses a fad   raise your privilege

if you're having a good time   our faces stuck

between the barriers of a dream   *save our future selves*

tomorrow's children   my son's favourite fruit needs to be washed

filling the jeep before a big drive   I've turned notifications off

I'm trying to limit what I become   wherever I end up next

I want to remember it   years back in L.A.   Hamza fired a gun

into the abdomen of white paper   his arms a loaded tremble

     on the ride home I said *we're the only species on earth*

with crooked teeth   laughing in our brand-new English   outside

the abattoir air stayed perfumed   by now we'd broken everything

that didn't need breaking   I can't stop

chewing on the city's loose vein   saline flags billowing in the countryside

over the post-war council estates   you wasted my dead's best habits

& it's only Tuesday

I'm scrolling through & every time it's this

honeyed blood carrying a coffin towards a pulse

Territory Two

Chapter 7

Though I am glad to be among the bitumen in a city
whose occupants resemble me & live as themselves

To say that this craze of identity has been purposely
cultivated for the podium, to smuggle me across the border

For aping European customs suspended over a terrace house,
garbed in St George ephemera, sneering at my enemies' sunburn

And manners is at present to focus on this little island as I know it
which voted against my natives, snatching air from a lifeboat's lung

Confined to the larger coastal towns who keep tidy pantries filled
with dolma, halloumi, a youngest on eBay bidding on keffiyehs

And there only among a certain class will you feel what it's like
to be made for populism, centrist voting & Aerospace Hawks

Middlemen and shopkeepers barristers drowning with St Mark's
Basilica – help me perform better, teach me the true genome of hatred

And in the more remote villages show me how to drink the peasant's
moonshine, rename his arthritic goat, alleviate the burden

In the interior of the island the grass cracks green & proper, faces pale
as those of crusaders, clean with citizenship mixed with their aura

The natives are unspoilt and hardly changed as if history has been
on its feet for too long; as road sweeper, toilet attendant, junior nurse

From their earlier ancestors who failed to remain, to keep their bows
out of Ireland – Nanking – Surat – the Royal Highland Regiment

asking *where are the forests? who owns this land? Look! Natives! Unshod*
stepping out the nave to capsize statues *in their mode of living.*

I

Circuitry

by the end of April I was trying my
best not to spill any more
electricity over my cortex. pacing
the old Roman road. stockpiling
litter. trapped inside synapses.
begging my brutality to go easy on
me. the circle I want to be loved by
looks like it's haemorrhaging
cortisol. wetlands of blood sugar.

inside fire what you get is fire. my
left amygdala is too small. my
mother's survival was too small. if
experiences shape the brain's
circuitry then I learned to fear the
father before the arachnid. my
deficit has been shipped to the
Kyrenia mountains – a tribe of
laundered goats to pay off God.

I'll fantasise about setting colonial summer houses alight with dendrites. I want so much of the past gone I'm terrified of moving. all around the therapist's chair I'm setting down my finery. his pencil outlining three letters I'm now obsessed by. in the next life I'll be better equipped to behead axons

with a Montblanc pen. write my son's name on thalamus glands. it's always urchins in the belly for dinner. a mouth like a seahorse before dawn. I like where I live now I'm just not big on the way I do it. thumbing quicker through my notebooks: *Has the best already happened?*

next door they're planning to build a conservatory from old money – life needs to colonise land. my earliest memory? throwing clumps of grey matter into the Mediterranean's basin then waiting for something substantive to return. at the Vietnamese restaurant my friends appear

so perfect in their simplicity.
laughing at futures full of morning
glory.

dopamine immigrating from their
polo necks.

an archipelago of adrenaline
withstanding the crush. calling us
in.

spark by gentle spark.

Endgame

at the close of capitalism catch the professor & I
waving our big flags at the parade

our haircuts inspired by Barthes's coinage
gusts of life

seniors leaning out of windows
their imminent deaths a thing of the past

that's me in the corner suffering conclusions
that's me itching to sing my killers to sleep

leaving them supine in a retro spa

All Together Now as if we were smuggling winter
into Dartmoor as if this were a collective effort

to find the oath I buried inside a chapel organ

the professor read how my mother thought to smother
the hour I was born in   you're right, I'm reaching

beyond the pablum for a straw man to leave my plasma
on   muscled colonies so saccharine I could die

All Together Now as if we were the study of a pale body
tanning in unison

it's not life we want more of, it's beauty

these days you can watch the world soften in high
definition

     watch a man fire into a crowd
     until the man becomes a government

my grandmother dug up the last of her savings
then went on to fill her purse

     the cicadas are screaming to know
why their singular music moves me to the point of vapour

     the professor believes the future is undergoing
     its final autopsy

     isn't that why the highest-grossing movies
     always contain some kind of high-speed chase?

& why most conversations between strangers
begin with the mention of weather

     which in itself is a kind of light

Versive Diagnosis

fog attempts to describe a hill. me. the skinny kid who never looked fully before crossing. icicle black tongue. penny-sweet buzz. asking if the singer was dead at the end of each classic.

who asked & asked. who ruined too many wedding receptions. I'm best kept in my ruins. bombed to the point I'm unable to pronounce the only thing my parents agreed on. how much of this is conditioned?

I'm here squandering a wage on talk therapy & discounted hallelujahs. a genuine *class act* devoted to alacrity & hero worship. my great grandfather sitting upright in a torn photograph.

looking so damn God. I'm writing this island guilt into something *dark & sexy*. see me before I cash you in. before my dead grandmother's only diamond thong dries up on the almighty's porch.

my situation looks so certain I'm wearing it like a city. chemo boils my spunk nomadic. in the hard of Caravaggio's brush my dead grandfather's pubic bone sticks to history's throat.

sweet oily Jesus how much of this was you
on me? listen, I can hear my old man going off on one again. the incoming winds
of Abyssinia. Carthage. Babylon. Europe.
Hackney.

Quotidian Theory

Da Silva suggests the death of God
gave birth to four white men

    Appiah has it as the Battle of Tours

I'm re-reading Rankine
75.8% of Puerto Ricans self-identify as white

at lunch I share the quote with P
who removes his Zanna Bukar cap

suppose   I say   referencing
Linda Alcoff *selves are*
constituted in relationship to communities
that have been racially constructed

    what then happens when there are multiple
    conflicting communities through which a self
    is constituted?

we split the bill   check to see if it's raining
        before becoming more
        East London

– so who are the four white men?

Sussman has it as
Grant – Davenport – Osborn – Laughlin –

each attempted to monopolize anthropology
in the early 20th century

but can racism & its apparatus
be accurately documented?

Uighur	Rohingya
Kashmir	Armenia
Palestine	Sudan
Yemen	Sámi

history is here, happening to us

    are we not all predisposed to at least
some degree of tribalism   ?   discuss: as in
whose life matters more   your mother's
or the stranger's toppled by a sparrow?
         I've read about historical persecution
of the Chinese   I've written
a paper on East Timor
            that Darwin quote
or was it
      Baldwin   probably Baldwin
I think all theories are suspect

what's AmericaBritain's greatest fear?

on the green A asks why I even care.
after all, she says, *I could pass if I wanted*

at the end of Ronald Storrs's
Orientations he observes the Cypriot
noting

I understand a white & black gentleman
but these inbetweens I do not want to understand

I cite the opening of Charif Shanahan's
poem 'Asmar'   I get tired of carrying

the beating my grandfather inherited
the Great Britain my father inherited
my mother inherited my brother inherited
my sister working against my father's
inheritance my father his father's mother
gets tired of carrying

I pull at the grass   witness a cloud
vomit a pair of ostrich feathers
                  recall a line
from the critic who reviewed my book
Violence and its Children –

Maggie Nelson's *The Art of Cruelty*
examines the work of performance artist
Nao Bustamante who said *I really encourage you*
          to leave your body

I'm having a conversation with R
regarding the way a body is rendered
through a public imagining   who gets to speak
on behalf of the body etc.

    & carry it all the way home   who decides
which body can leave   which body can stay
how will a body become seen

    or heavy enough to sleep   marvellous enough to fuck
understanding itself in the life of itself

    whose body gets to pirouette
    whose body makes a perfect target
whose body is kept awake by the body politic

I'm alive in Great Britain   I'm alive

so who's that lying next to me?

around the wooden table there's some talk

I don't know about the you or me they keep
referring to but my country is split between
this & that   composed of distances
a border bill   ok I take pleasure in exploiting
my emergencies

imagine this amount of knowing
& still a child grows into a question.

in Paul Bloom's *Against Empathy* he writes
Empathy is limited in that it focuses on specific individuals.
Its spotlight nature renders it innumerate and myopic.

I'm back round the wooden table for the last time
where we make our requests. so far each week
the menu has been different.

my son asked why we shoot to kill the only
species that fly – *is that why they invented*
gods & superheroes?   (sweet kid).

if you're serious take off the falconry glove
to feel how the raptor really has it.

For Those Who Demand Evidence

what I wouldn't give to turn silent today
to lead the frontline of language towards
the cliff dropping my sad mornings
beside some gentle accident it's my
friends I'm thinking of dead inside
their faultless bodies offering up ground
I'll donate a modicum of hard cash to
the approaching circus two fatigued
elephants carting heirlooms rebranding
this new age vacuum packed conscious-
ness I wish I could play an instrument
on days like today a stoned pianist with
poor posture forfeiting moral hands
for the freedom of a chord I swear to
be part of anything that sees me I can't
stress this enough a famous past stole
our homes my family survived empire
a violence to my father's head I was only
a boy then with squeaky clean shoes
his pants all sullied now I'm paying
institutions to read up on what was
originally mine ripping body parts off
eugenicists bigots preserved in specimen
jars England I've spent so long inside
your history it's like there will never be
another way round this black torch held
between your fangs clapping at the end
of an American movie how do we stop
let love move us naturally dodge another
set knee the weight of our dead one last
plea what I wouldn't give to turn silent

today before statistics catch a siren
turn into a baton swinging meat slave
roads shimmying under brute force
the second coming down above his
temple her pelvis cracking law into
order forced to beg a badge says what
it wants my friends lost to daylight
appearances a platoon of cameras
my country your country rolling like
jackals thick with a sickness for blood
blond blue white

II

Across from Here

where I began, for argument's sake, let's call it love
each day pinned to the next, my mother
when using my father's name would know what to do
with us, & him, far away in an unlit capital
already falling further into his glasses, our kitchen table, minus
his rage – a column missing its figure – where I first said aloud father
or dad, or sir, or nation to a blank seat, a white plate
one mottled prune, the severed leg of our cat. so let's say
for argument's sake, I was a good boy looking for my father
in songs or movies or the house of my childhood which burnt
down the last day of summer – a whole family died – my mother
saying it's fine for boys to feel terrible & ruined alone
in life which ends up infecting us all, & God knows why
it's sod's law, we find ourselves whispering father
into the side of a pillow, a boy's head cracked open
his ears leaking *father* all over the canteen floor,
unswept crumbs, a mirror under the bed, two shot
pheasants by the sink waiting for my mother. the day he returned
father left my mouth differently. I started to declare
words no longer mine, catchphrases dead inside their box
the meaning of father never looked back to check
I was still there; over time some words come close
to disappearing, kept alive only by the people who repeat them,
father, for argument's sake, let's call it love where I began

Comber

in this one a woman stands by the eastern shoreline
it's not clear if she's fully clothed   her mask wilting
the way my sister's will   she holds out
an unassuming hand the way a woman in a movie might
to ensure a laconic man's safety her fingers complete with dark
rings her feet slowly drugged by the rapids   she's smiling
I'm smiling without needing to know why
I consider life inside her lungs swelling a neon white
seven more waves fashioned by obsidian cavort around her ankles
by now it's unclear if she's walking backwards
or if the sea is levying the land   either way
she appears to be shrinking amid the plastic bottle necks
loose continents & smoke tops – I feel myself heating
inside the idea – I panic looking for the next junction
turning over   a new sea erupts   now there's only marl
sandstorm & legislation   she shakes me   throws
a metal detector my way but it won't leave the thistle bush
it can't turn off

Mother Myth

we're at the point where my mother counts veils inside her age. arranging baby photos & fallen teeth like rows of sweet garlic. I want to do right under the remains of her life. to sit & attend a thought she's struggling to satisfy. my brother says she needs a stronger constitution. a more committed world view. two carafes of baptismal wine. a few more seconds to unclamp my ego – I survived the result. managed to forgive what remained of my teenage predilections.

I'm climbing through her memory like a stone. marking her wrists with iron dowels *one year you know, we were so poor we had to share splinters – oh you were a bad kid, never could sit still.* I'm back with the woodlice & jackdaws. peasants who worshipped crickets with purple clay in their blood. my whole life I've been working to reach the five-fingered mountain to watch my closest myth die. one sea anemone for luck. my mother's imprint on a dry massif.

the room radiated rosemary & urine. I arrived in good faith. a broken clock on a Persian veranda. towards the end, my myth had nothing left to exonerate. clearing away her body. folding down her wrinkles. with my right hand I resurrected what persisted – *I'm sorry.* held back a final thank you. (I'm talking about my living mother again.) the apogee shrinking to umbilicus rind. her pulse two loose buttons on a boy's winter coat. her pulse my childhood as it was.

I took all I could carry back down. from the top there was little left. a bouquet to place by her window. the long grey membrane of hospitals. this is all yours to pass on: once upon a life my myth decided to wear another man's voice for safety. promise I'll keep a tin of Cyprus olives inside my lifeboat. douse my son's bedsheets in eucalyptus. never will I turn my back on the thrum. to allow a version of anti-history to get away. your glasses brought up close.

white moved from off your face. balm for your lips. ok ready. can you look to where my finger points? μαμά – can you look towards your son? μαμά – his face like a satellite you can blast right out of orbit.

On Leave Until

nothing died today & by that I mean progress. all around the city people were in love with their fractures. their exacting marrow. I caught the retired exec leave an eyelash on his competitor's palm.

steel buckets confessed to the names of last year's cultivars. the terminally ill stroked the whale bone of their deaths. wombs of ewes rolled from fridge freezers. gulls spun in their oil spills like ancient fish.

I thought I'd send a message to my mother. by that I mean a message to myself. my father replied with his symmetry so the day was spent wondering if the work of blood was valued by the aorta.

before bed my little empire wrapped his arms around my neck. I made a lullaby out of the ways I'd been hunted. by the end we were fast asleep. our wheezing the allegorical labour of tomorrow.

III

Squib

I started life as dead currency. in the first week of spring a male voice on the radio said children develop a taste for praise by frightening off birds. as an adult I've been attending to myself in my finest faux leather. rocking the old days like a proto-meme. a subdued pleat. a Neolithic aphorism. I finished this bestseller in one day: *Ways We Should All Be Breathing* – it proposed I forgive my past for its stubbornness so I'll sneak the leading probiotic into the tabernacle while six hooded men edit the bio of Christ. my skull needs lathering before it bribes the priest's sniper scope, which started out as liquid sand relying solely on the glassblower's breath.

these days I'm all epigenetics & indignation. minarets & oneiric miracles. I'm bending over backwards to kiss my trauma's forehead – all furrowed. as if it were my only son dreaming of being believed by the tea in a gaiwan. the job of any parent is to prepare their children for a world without them. fear is the only conclusive list. I remember the body mass index of each Byzantine saint. the mosque across the road looks so peaceful. so photogenic. a public address blunders into barrier tape. since then I've made it a habit to check the ingredients of my opening gambits. weaponising certainty. the glittered spool of a life wound –

Float

The chance to be part of this happens briefly:
my son grows to edge where the ocean slips, roughly
pointing towards a float,   he asks
me to rescue it from a future he can't see –
three slow steps in until I'm governed by cold
moving towards an unknown confluence. I'll say

how I panicked, unmoored by my weight. they say
the closer you get to time the further it moves, for a brief
second I believed I could make a difference, another cold
thought splits my side   salt clings, feels rough
around my limits, each wave dumping sweat. I see
my son's worry in the surge, hear his asking

rumble through the earth's bladder, I want to ask
for more time. how can a body reverse in water? I say
aloud *I don't think I'll make it*   seeing
his profile plunge like a conch. as a boy I took a brief
diving course where I learnt how oxygen turns starfish rough
drying them into land until a child discovers the cold

of them, chucking what's left into a bucket. over time our colder
selves arrive to find us struggling against the drift, asking
for a cup of moonlight to sunny the medals from our rougher
years.   say
I persevered, not wanting him to see me fail, even if for a brief
second he lost sight of me or believed I drowned at sea –

I'll stay repurposing my strongest lines, see
the float reaching for my hand, the gap becoming less cold,
reminding me the ocean is alive inside the world; its brief
to keep the retina saline, to not need a question, asking
for little in return. the sea: it refuses to say
why it keeps down the masthead, the ghost roughly

the size of my son's waiting. I turn towards him roughly
where I left, what's keeping me afloat? my work sees
him dressing up for a life, rehearsing what I'll finally say
hill-walking out the ocean his float in hand, juddering from cold
I did it for you   I'll declare   if he ever asks
where I was the whole time then I'll keep my explanation brief

roughly the way my father did during those colder years
when I begged his hand to turn me calm. I'm looking across the foreshore.
I can't see him anywhere. I had this to give. to say briefly.

Structuralism

I'll make the sky do something it's never done, like scratch its ear
before bending over a rockpool.

I'll make it spread itself wide as smoke watching how it's grabbed by
carp in sediment, backslapping with the force of a hook into a courtroom, the undertow turning its light away.

I'm deep inside my convictions courtesy of these big machines, typing
as if I know what you're incapable of knowing, thinking about next
year when every school will become a custody room.

from outside my oak door I'll clap extremely loud on the cul-de-sac
I inherited, dreaming about the aforementioned   *how hard they can
work to stimulate economic growth* . . . that scrounging piece of sky
taking up space.

I'll make sure the sky happens – heading towards a future nobody
asked for. from my gondola I read reports of a tower at capacity, my
grandad's council tower, families demolished beneath a presidential
suite, my foreign body a tourist obsessed with hot water.

by my window a nation applauds from the flare of its border. there is
no more aid, militia coerce gardenias seconds before a bomb explodes
ruining a covey of quails   a hospital for children who lay very still
                        children who should only be that still when playing

hide & seek. the centre page shows a man who resembles my uncle but
is not, looking up at the same patch of cloud as yesterday – his stare a
whole line of earthquakes.

gently
the children
have been washed
& scented against
their will.
so thick
the salt of dogs.
air is the hardest
thing of all.
I want us to share
orange socks.
heavy coats. washing
lines. & windpipes.
a whole bandwagon.
to stay still
during the ads.
time taking us both.
holding our cheeks
to the bruise our fathers
left. I know.
you know.
this page you're
talking into.
the hunger you want
to choke. man.
look how fucking
vegan we are. cooler
& more dangerous
than an uncooked
egg. how nearly
dead we were.

an adult lying
to a child is bedtime.
the other way round
is war.
who drilled
these fractions
into us? who stood
by & watched?
I want to tell you
it'll all be fine. as
though any of us
last. make it past
the final if

through
   the window
      another window
         smaller than it was
            inside a family appear
               to settle around a continent

in the middle they lump a mixed
language together the way families
do when the window is clear a dog below
the rear gable licks its paw worries through its
tongue I have forgotten the breed what I'm really
waiting for is to see who'll be first to grin the mother
prepares the father his assortment of meats the children
know very little about childhood the dog keeps licking its paw
I know something is about to happen to the small boy who hasn't
said a word since the last time he mumbled stop father makes sure
he's done with his meats before taking a final swig I'm still waiting for
an uncle or aunty to rush in to release the family from the bonds of love
the daughter prods her peas with a breadstick the dog will not stop licking
its paw the mother opens a tin of tuna cuts her fourth finger as the boy walks
towards the window miming a phrase – I raise my hand to my mouth as sure as a
harp needing to land alive saying *I see you boy* I'm coming to turn the sound
on all the good people know about you but the dog will not stop licking
its paw the father lifts his body forcing apart the violence of borders
marching towards the small boy who by now has nothing left to
say I grab the stool hurling it straight through the window
looking at my life as though I need reminding arms out
I jump into my father who's busy gargling his prime
I'll hold his left hand until I'm out the door in a
country with a boy standing by a window
smaller than it was inside

a family settle around a
continent next door the odour
is like a grave hurled through
the window becoming a throat
living inside the noise
it attempted to make

❀

NOTES

'Heritage Aesthetics' borrows lines from *The Ending of Time* by J. Krishnamurti and Dr David Bohm (1985).

'Perhaps, a Rhetoric' is a found poem using extracts taken from Lawrence Durrell's *Bitter Lemons of Cyprus* (1958).

'Endgame' borrows the phrase 'gusts of life' from Roland Barthes, *Mourning Diary*.

'We Are Us Now' uses an epigraph from *The Grenadier*, a magazine issued to guards stationed on British Cyprus. As quoted in *Legacy of Strife: Cyprus from Rebellion to Civil War* by Charles Foley (1962).

'Circuitry' incorporates research around anxiety disorders outlined in *Rewire Your Anxious Brain: How to Use the Neuroscience of Fear to End Anxiety, Panic and Worry* by Catherine M. Pittman and Elizabeth M. Karle (2015).

The opening line in 'Float' is quoted from Guy Burgs, as heard in the song 'Burgs' by Mt. Wolf.

In 'Mother Myth' the 'five-fingered mountain' is a reference to the Pentadactylos mountain range in northern Cyprus, or Beshparmak in Turkish, or Five Fingered Mountain in English. The mountains are home to one of the oldest Cypriot myths in which a villager falls in love with a local queen. The queen orders the villager to fetch her holy water from the monastery of St Andreas (an arbitrary request) before she can agree to marry him. When the villager returns successfully, the queen becomes furious and refuses to marry him. Angered by her dishonesty the villager picks up a handful of mud to throw at her. The queen dodges the throw, causing the mud to travel towards the mountain range. The lasting imprint that looks like five fingers is said to be what remains of the villager's rage.

'*Though I am glad to be among the bitumen in a city*' uses found text from photographer Basil Stewart when he visited Cyprus between

1905 and 1906, to document life on the island. Republished in *The Island of Cyprus, A Photographic Itinerary from the 19th to the 20th Century* (2007).

'Quotidian Theory' uses ideas and arguments found in the following texts: Denise Ferreira da Silva, *Toward a Global Idea of Race* (2000); Kwame Anthony Appiah, *The Lies that Bind: Rethinking Identity* (2018); Claudia Rankine, *Just Us: An American Conversation* (2020); Linda Alcoff's essay 'Mestizo Identity' published in Robert Bernasconi and Tommy L. Lott, *The Idea of Race* (2000); Robert Sussman, *The Myth of Race* (2014); Ronald Storrs, *Orientations* (1939); Charif Shanahan, *Into Each Room We Enter Without Knowing* (2017); Maggie Nelson, *The Art of Cruelty: A Reckoning* (2011); Paul Bloom, *Against Empathy* (2017).

ACKNOWLEDGEMENTS

Thank you to these minds who each had critical input, generous instruction and words of assurance along the writing road: Rachael Allen – Jack Underwood – Wayne Holloway-Smith – Claudia Young – Will Harris – Nikesh Shukla – Joelle Taylor – Tom MacAndrew – Karim Kamar – Sam Bromfield – Sabrina Mahfouz – Tabari Mahfouz-Anaxagorou – Sandeep Parmar – Emily Berry – Inua Ellams – André Naffis-Sahely – Mona Arshi – Nick Makoha – Bahriye Kemal – Daniele Nunziata – Arianna Koudounas – Ilaeira Leto Agrotou Georgiou – Reuben Christian – Phivos Christofides – Syima Aslam – Akala – Patricia Ferguson – Mum – Dad – brother – sister – cousins – those carried over.

Thank you to Granta Books – Greene & Heaton – Arts Council England – Poetry School – First Story – Southbank Centre – Bradford Literature Festival – Spread the Word – Poet in the City – Bedtime Stories for the End of the World.

Thank you to the Society of Authors who awarded me an Authors' Foundation Grant, specifically an Arthur Welton Award in memory of the poet and philanthropist, which afforded me vital time to work on the poems during the pandemic.

Thank you also to the editors of the following magazines where several of these poems first appeared: *'we'd been in Algiers'* and 'On Leave Until' in the *London Magazine*; 'At the Centre a House' in *Poetry Wales*; *'what a time to be alive'* (formerly titled 'Grounded') in the *New Statesman*; 'Futurist Primer' in the *Poetry Review*; 'Heritage Aesthetics' in *Poetry London*; 'Text Message' in *Poetry* (Chicago); 'Circuitry' in *MIT Technology Review*; 'Endgame', '15 × 22' and 'My Weapons Are Working People' in *Five Dials*; *'gently the children'* (formerly titled 'Washing Lines & Windpipes') in the *Adroit Journal*; 'Structuralism' in *Bath Magg*.

'Squib' was commissioned by the Bradford Literature Festival and made into a stop-motion film by One 6th Animation. It won first place in the poetry category of The Motion Picture International Film Festival 2021.

'Mother Myth' was commissioned by Bedtime Stories for the End of the World.

'*gently the children*' is dedicated to my friend Wayne Holloway-Smith.

'Across from Here' was first published in the 2020 Creative Futures Award anthology.